what if our love stories
are not about our lovers
but are the tales
of how we found ourselves

The Evolution of a Girl

First Printing, 2018
ISBN-13: 978-0692144046
ISBN-10: 0692144048

Dedicated to

Courtney for inspiring my heart,
Kathryn for inspiring my spirit,
and my mother
for cultivating a foundation rich enough for me to grow.

Illustrations by Marie Worden

Fighting. Climbing. Rising.
Dirt in her throat and her spirit suddenly
too much
for her skin.

The air. The sun. The trees;
where she makes her final ascent
and sings.

The Girl

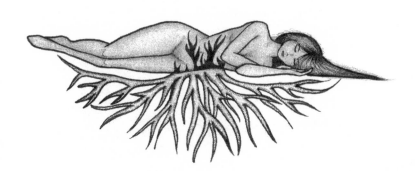

Young. Naïve.
A bud breaking through the security of the ground.
The world.
Open. Daunting.
An expanse where fairytales ring true;
where the only endeavor is acquiring the love of a man.
Sex means love.
Rejection means insignificance.
Existence teeters on the edge of his lips.

L.E. Bowman

desperation clung to me like perfume

love me

love me

love me

You knew my heart
would never find a home
within your chest,
and still
you invited me in.

Her childhood didn't teach her what it meant to be wanted.
She never learned that lips weren't only for yelling;
that hands could actually be kind.
So when his lips felt warm on her body,
and his hands were coarse but steady,
she didn't know how
to not open;
didn't know how
to not beg him
to come inside.

maybe we give our hearts away
because we believe
even the harshest of hands
are more tender
than our own

He compliments my body
with the same coolness and persistence
as the wind in the fall.
And I can tell by the way
his eyes
boldly dance
through my limbs,
that he expects I will shed myself
with the same willingness and grace
as the trees.

Make him chase you,
my grandmother told me.
Keep that desire tucked between your thighs.
Give him something to find.

You said
I should be thankful;
that only pretty girls
make men
want them like that.
But when you said pretty,
you meant sexy.
And when you said wanted,
you meant
would do anything to have.

My head was dizzy and my center ached.
Unbalanced.
Off-kilter.
The world spinning backwards,
or was it even spinning at all?
That means you've been rammed good,
the girls were laughing.
I suppose I was laughing too;
it echoed in my head along with my thoughts.
My back hurts.
Oh yes,
the remnants of carpet,
and my skin burned where his fingers had touched.
I could still hear the sounds of the party;
see faint lights flickering along the bottom of the door.
The taste of whiskey.
The scent of salt.
Maybe it was all my doing;
I remembered moans
—they were his
but I couldn't remember saying
no.

These emotions feel like foreign invaders
    marching to my gut.
    bombing my heart.
    firing in my lungs.
I fight until my palms are sweaty;
until my throat is choked with the remnants
of all the tiny battles
I swear I have won.

I think that is the difficult part,
to wage a war
within yourself;
to breathe the smoke,
feel the burning in your throat.
And amidst the flames and cries of anguish,
you watch as the world
keeps turning,
as the sun comes up,
as everything around you
moves on.

did you hate
that part of you
before someone told you
you should

I was born loving myself.

It wasn't until others already polluted with insecurities
began to point out the pieces of me they deemed
unbeautiful
that I began to see parts of me
as less.
I didn't see my breasts as small
until a boy
told me that they were.
I didn't see my frame as frail
until fingers
poked and prodded the bones at my hips.
I didn't see my nose as damaged
until voices
told me I should get it fixed.
I am no longer whole,
but parts and pieces
put into categories
of satisfactory and flawed.

My words feel heavy
on my tongue,
but as soon as they leave my lips
they turn to feathers.

Delicate.

Easily crushed.

Easily lost,

and scattered.

maybe i should tell you
i love you
and let the words
rest on your lips
instead of clinging
to mine

I love hard. Embarrassingly hard. All in type of hard.

But I do so silently.

I drown the feelings in my gut until I am heavy with *I want you* and
I love you and *I miss you*. I hold my hope in my throat where his lips should
rest. I clutch my wishes in my hands where his fingers belong.

They become moist with sweat until I no longer want them.

The knowing is easy.
It is
the not knowing
that will tear you apart.

I have no balance
in love.
I either guard my heart completely,
or I toss it away.

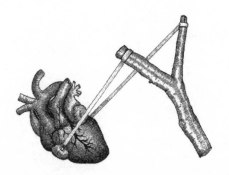

This is your doing.
This natural disaster.
This eruption on the inside.
This earthquake beneath my skin
when my heart shifts
and suddenly
my body
can't help but move.

You only wanted me at 3:00am
    proof enough of your intentions,
but I was so willing to forgo parts of myself
just to hold you
that I painted
all your red flags
white.

Do not mistake passion for love.

One feeds you;
the other leaves you starving.

I knew the truth. the depth.
of my desires
would scare you,
so I forced my needs to be silent;
I buried my wants behind a guise of indifference.
I allowed something
that should feed me
to consume me
until I felt nothing
but empty. and starving.

i was nude before you
but not naked

He will come back
as he always does.
Lonely nights and cold mornings,
looking for a body
   —any body
and I will open my arms or my legs
    sometimes neither
    typically both
and I will pretend to have the situation
under control.
Because I can easily open my arms or my legs,
and keep my heart closed.
These lies I tell myself
    sometimes neither
    typically both.

My hands
were too soft.
My thighs
too warm.
I felt too much like home
for a man only looking to fill
a casual vacancy.

We were trapped between
I don't need you
and
I can't live without you.
That horrible place
where nothing ends.

Where nothing truly begins.

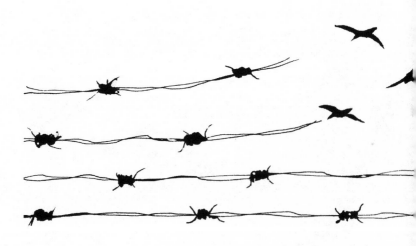

it seems perfect now
in the stillness of morning
but at some point
one of us
will have to
move

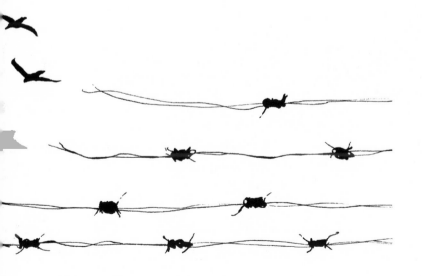

I remember your breath on my neck,
your groans in my ear.
The wet warmth
before your body moved from mine;
before a towel appeared at my face.
The cold came quickly then;
the realization
that an act,
something so intimate and warm,
cold leave me feeling
so cold and insecure.

— Clean yourself

a man will tell you
all of his truths
but you must be
silent enough
to listen
and brave enough
to hear

He was levity.

And I used to wonder
why I always felt
so beautifully
torn.

He was gravity.

Please don't ask
because you know the answer will be
yes.
And then where will we be?
You
with pieces
I'm not sure you ever wanted.
And me
wondering
which part I gave you this time,
and if I can manage
to live
without ever getting it back.

Naked.
Newly alone.
The heat still pulsing between my thighs.
Quiet tears silenced by heavy breaths.
Finally knowing
no matter how many times I ask him to see me
    all of me
not just the physical being he occupies regularly,
but the woman.
the heart.
the mind.
I will always be a means of escape,
    a vessel
and the ending will always be the same;

                  with him in the shower washing me away.

Give me honesty.
Give me grief.
Give me heartbreak.

Just do not give me silence.

I thought it would be louder,
    the moment
a person falls apart.
The shattering of hope.
The destruction of spirit.
How can an earthquake create
rubble
of an entire world,
and everyone around
only hear
silence?

the true pain of loneliness
is not the absence of other people
but the inescapable presence
of yourself

Something is unraveling,
and I don't know if it is
you or me
or us.
But I can hear
the threads tearing.
I can feel the tangles
as they pull apart.
And I keep reaching and grasping and pulling,
but all I end up with
are fingers
stained
with what little remains
of our hearts.

we broke each other
because it hurt
less
than letting go

You call me needy
as the remnants
of the last fruit you devoured
drip.
   down.
      your.
         chin.
How many trees have you left
barren.
harmed.
How many times
have they given
while you only
take?

It's about the consumption;
    the plucking.
The holding perfection in your hands
and knowing
you
will be the one
to taint it.

— *Purity*

If you are torn between
staying and going

—go.

I want a lover
who knows.

You call this love?
This allowing me to drown
while I struggle to keep you
above water.

I knew it was coming;
the way his voice remained calm. No rise. No fall.
Steady.
Cool.
Collected.
Planned words pouring from practiced lips.
It's for the best. The timing just isn't right.
The words sunk into my chest.
Heavy.
Foreboding.
It was not the pain of another ending; the fear of having to start again.
It was the knowing.
The knowing that this was not a case of souls not connecting.
This was one woman—open.
    ready.
and one man
terrified to let her in.

the people who leave you
with more questions than answers
are the people
who fear the answers
themselves

L.E. Bowman

I no longer know
if it's your voice I keep hearing,
or if it's even
your scent
that still clings to my skin.
Maybe you're now
more fantasy
than memory.
Just a collection
of wants
I poured into a man.

You were not making love to me.
You were carving your name
into my bones.

And I used to wonder why it hurt.

My hands are open.
My arms are closed.
But my bones
my bones
still quiver
at the thought of you.

Happiness
feels like water leaking through my fingers.
I try to catch it,
but it splashes and escapes and soaks into the ground.
I try to pinpoint
when I stopped collecting it in buckets;
when I became content
just watching it puddle at my feet
with the waste and the wreckage
and all the other debris.

Apathy moved in like an unwelcome houseguest.
I saw the remnants of its occupation
on once pure floors and vibrant walls;
    untidy halls
I could no longer keep clean.

the loneliest place
i have ever been
is in love

I wish
just once
that the world would actually end
when my heart did.
That I would wake up
and there wouldn't be the sun and the birds and the sky.
Instead
the haze of my mind would surround me;
the despair and the pain dark tendrils in my eyes.
But here I am again,
another morning without you,
and I can still hear
those cackling birds
and see
that bastard light.

It isn't the strike that hurts;
it's the surviving.
The cut of the shards the first breath after.
The realizing
that through all the pain,
you must somehow learn
how to breathe
again.

how can i feel
so on fire
with this water
pouring
from my skin

I learned from my father
that the ache
can consume us.
That weak people
break others
to keep themselves together,
and even good men
sometimes
walk away.

How much weight that must be;

all those lies
you carry.

L.E. Bowman

the woman in me
gracefully
let you go
but the animal in me
was howling and tearing at my skin

You aren't in love,
my mother said.
Love isn't twists and turns
in the gut.
It isn't shaking hands
and hearts that forget how to beat.
Love is steady,
my mother said.
Guts.
Hands.
Beats.
It's the ginger you take when you're unsettled.
It's the rhythm you cling to when the song around you
begins to change.

L.E. Bowman

We are all born with the instinct.
The ability to hear the trees;
to taste the wind.
Our feet so covered in earth
it looked like we sprang from it.
We knew how to run,
how to cry,
when to sit in silence and when to growl.

But that all ends with a cage;
smiling and laughing we walk in.
Look we say,
I am not a child anymore.
Look,
I have tamed myself with muzzles and razor blades.
Look,
there is no longer dirt on my skin.

I can still hear the roar of the cicadas;
feel the sweat sliding down my back.
My slick thighs.
My pounding chest.
The hunger was raw then;
    open.
    needy.
The earth could feel it,
and the trees screamed it back to me.

I'm not living;
I'm surviving.
My lungs doing nothing but pushing and pulling air.
My fingers are breaking,
but it isn't earth I'm digging.
My stomach is growling,
but it isn't food I need.

We put ourselves behind walls.
Close windows.
Lock doors.
And then hate the sun
for not asking to come in.

L.E. Bowman

then i realized
you only had power over me
because i gave it to you

You were a lesson;
the difference between
attraction and compatibility.
Want and need.
Everything
I was starving for,
and nothing
that could feed me.

Don't call it love
just because you fought so hard
to keep it.
That's wanting more than loving.
Pulling things to your chest
that never belonged there.
Holding them tight.
Hating them when they fight to leave.
Hating yourself
when you can't
make them stay.

The danger is rarely
the other person.
The danger is
yourself.

How far
you are willing to go.
How many ways
you are willing to break.

At some point
my body won't ache for yours,
and my hands will feel full without your fingers around them.

At some point
I will hear your voice or smell your skin,
and I will still be able to think and feel and move.

At some point
I will have a new lover (*or no lover*),
and will sing along to love songs without your name
drowning out the words.

But first I have to miss you.
But first I have to learn to let you go.
But first I have to relearn how to hold myself alone.

I was a forest after a fire.
Smoldering.
Desolate.
And ready
to grow anew.

it does not matter
how well he loved you
if he was still willing
to let you go

Sometimes you miss it even more
when you never actually had it.
When your imagination does that thing
with the pedestal and perfection.
When you get ideas
of what the person is
or isn't.
When you never realize
that neither
are true.

She's just angry,
so angry.
And she condemns him for causing her pain.
She says the joints in her fingers bother her more
now that there's nothing to hold on to;
says she's empty without him around.
But I think the truth is,
she sold herself when she met him.
A soul to a devil;
a vacant hand thinking it had to have something to fill it.

A woman never realizing she could do it herself.

I guess in that sense,
she isn't lying.
With him gone,
she truly has
nothing
now.

Don't blame him
for breaking you.
He might
have made you cold,
but it was you
who clenched so hard
your pieces
shattered.

you know
you are in need
of yourself
when you begin ignoring the scratches and bruises
on your knees
because all you care about
is collecting
the little pieces of love
people tossed at your feet

I guess it isn't fair to blame you.

I kept
pouring myself into your palms
even as I watched
all that I was
leak through your fingers.

I reached and I grasped and I pulled,
but my hands remained empty.
I yearned and I pleaded and I waited
and still
I had nothing to show.

So I moved and I worked and I created
the life I wanted;
I stopped expecting the world
to give me what I thought
I was owed.

stop begging for table scraps
that will never fill you
that will only keep you
starving for more

—you deserve a seat at the table

L.E. Bowman

There is pain
in the letting go.
In the realization
that the person you love
is becoming
the person you loved.

Let go anyway.

You've been leaving for months it seems,
and yet you will not go.
Your bags are packed,
but you keep them near the closet.
You reach for the door,
but you always turn around,

and I'm gutted and weary and tired of waiting;

I'm the one
leaving you now.

I was lost in the dreams
others had for me;
struggling to create a life
I was never meant
to live.

it is difficult to reach
for the one
you know
you are becoming
while still grasping the hand
of the one
you were

The change comes when all that remains is your own skin;
your own bones.
When there is your heart and your mind,
and you can admit that they hate each other.
When you have no one left to blame
but yourself.

When you aren't quite sure if this is rock bottom,
but you feel like you've finally found
solid ground.

I felt thin
   in body.
   in soul.
A disappearing woman bloated with ideas but starving for self-love.
A beggar wanting to live,
not just survive.
A seeker finally realizing that the greatest gift existed within her chest,
not another's arms.

I felt thin
   in body.
   in soul.

But I was suddenly ready to feast.

Give it time.

That pain won't always be at the forefront
of your mind.
Your plates will shift.
New life will bubble up from the old;
a rich foundation
where fresh joy will take root,
spread,
and grow.

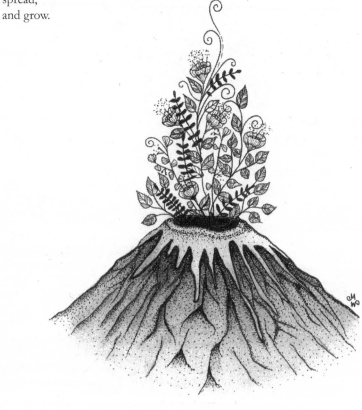

Accept it.
Embrace it.
Allow it to rip you apart.
Cry as it crawls through your skin.
For tomorrow is a new day,
and soon you will be free
to feel something
new.

darkness is a gift

it forces you to feel

Like leaves during autumn,
my fears and insecurities
cling to my limbs.
Slowly,
they illuminate and dry;
a beautiful death
that collects at my feet
in shades of amber and gold.

Newly bare, I await the spring.

The Evolution

With
a calm eye,
a sultry coolness,
she moves.
With
a violent temper,
a tempestuous spirit,
she consumes.
Like a storm,
she will engulf you.
Receive her,
and she will nourish you.
Challenge her,
and she will blow you away.

Trim your limbs
of broken twigs and dying leaves,
of rotting buds and cracking bark.
Allow the decay
to collect at your feet,
for flowers grow best
in fertile soil.

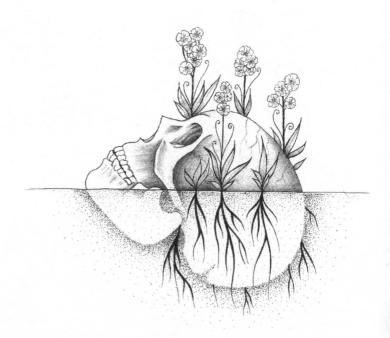

The world did not end
when we did.

And neither did I.

How am I
wonderful. beautiful. perfect.
but still not good enough to be with you?
Do not fill my head with lies to ease my pain.
Tell me my flaws,
so I may lavish them with love.
So I may show you
how the broken. the unhinged. the uncommon.
parts of me
are the most beautiful of all.

I am enough.

If you feel the need
to continue searching
between other women's thighs,
it is you
who is lacking.

What makes you think I owe you my breath?
The healing of my hands.
The pleasure of my thighs.
Who taught you a woman is an open door?
A place to crawl into when your ego needs tending;
when your fingers ache to grasp something
softer than your heart.
I know my body
looks generous
    inviting,
but this home and its warmth
are mine to share
not yours to claim.

—This body is my home, and I am asking you to leave.

I tried so hard
to make you fit,
but I am too much woman
to squeeze into a man
with such skinny ideals.

It was painful
the first time I told a man the truth;
the first time I vomited my wants
instead of choking on them.
The chunks
clung to my face and hands,
but they were out,
and I was finally
free.

I am still afraid
every day.

But there is joy
on the other side
of fear,
and I
have felt it.

Do not measure me by
the arch of my breast,
the slope of my waist,
the curve of my hip.
My shapes
might not fit your geometry,
but my heart and mind
are comprised of
more constellations and revelations,
more chemicals and miracles,
than your mathematical intellect
can comprehend.

you split me open
but i grew flowers
in the wounds

Did you think I couldn't sense
the dog in you?
Smell the whiskey and the smoke.
See the moon in your eyes.
Not all souls
are looking for salvation.
Some just want an animal
eager
to devour them
whole.

There is safety in falling
for wolves.
Unpredictable endings
are far more terrifying
than pain.

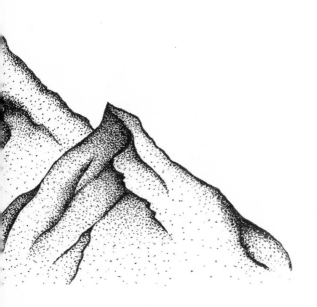

You are a harsh woman,
he said.
Maybe to you,
I replied.
I am most tender
early in the morning,

you just never stay to see.

he can speak
to your body
in beautiful tongues
but not know how
to tell your heart
good morning

Are you truly starving for me,
or are you just
attention starved?

Do not assume this body
feeds
any stray
hungering for a bite.

Yes.

I am earth
and water
and sun.
You can plant yourself
in the marrow of my bones,
and I can grow you.

But that doesn't mean
I should.

Or will.

I challenge you to taunt me.
I dare you to provoke me.
I might seem fragile,
but there is an animal
inside of me.
A creature
with an instinct to survive,
with a spirit
teetering
on the edge of wild.
Growling and pacing.
Pleading.
To be released.

i will wear bones in my hair
along with flowers
so you will know
even beautiful things
can be deadly

You claim you can please me
better than anyone,
but you forget
I have a vivid imagination
and two hands of my own.

I am not
the flower
in your suit jacket,
or the centerpiece
of your home.
I am not
still or crisp or fake.
I am
stems and petals and roots.
A field of blossoms.
That cannot be captured
or contained.

L.E. Bowman

Feminism came to me slowly.

The ember born in the way my parents raised me and ignited when I entered the workforce and realized professionalism didn't stop men from encouraging me to sit on their laps. It grew when the topic of my love life became more fascinating than my brain.

You aren't married?
Who will take care of you?
Don't you want to have kids?

It erupted when I realized that my life as a young woman was riddled with moments of sexism that went unnoticed until I awoke to the realities of everyday interactions. Unsolicited hands on my body. Laughing faces against my chest. Drinks tainted. Worth reduced to a number shouted by a bunch of frat boys. My self-love contaminated by the possibility that a man might not find me attractive.

Being afraid to say no—prude.
Being afraid to say yes—whore.

I am no longer blind to these moments, and I will continue to highlight their existence until the world sees the truth.

You joke about my body
being too much to handle.
Thighs and hips
too thick for your hands.
Ass and tits
too juicy for your mouth.
But boy
it isn't my body
you need to worry about.
It's my mind.

It will eat you alive.

he can admire your strength
and still
want to break you

Women are encouraged to remain small;
expected to be delicate creatures
with closed legs and disappearing waists.
With voices only heard when spoken to,
and opinions only shared when asked.
With sexual urges felt but not explored,
and sensuality seen but not exploited.
To be anything less is lacking.
To be anything more is overbearing;
is dominating.
Is too powerful;
too beautiful.
For society;
for men.
to control.

— *Be so much more that they don't know what to do with you.*

L.E. Bowman

Civilized?

Please.

Like we no longer
claw and scavenge and sift
through the shit.
Like we aren't vultures
pretending to be lions.
Like we aren't savages
with self-made crowns.

We spend so much time running from ourselves.
Scared of the heat.
The hunger.
The stench under our arms.
The callouses on our hands.
We hide the signs of living
like we aren't all yearning for the chance
to actually
be free.

All aggressive dogs have stories,
origins of pain.
Sculpted from flesh and muscle and pounding hearts
by hands
that beat and break.
A mimicry of their creator's masculinity;
a symbol of their master's strength.
Kicked and twisted and taunted
until all affronts are met with violent rage.
These damaged egos.
These once pure hearts.
These innocents
grown
from fear and hate.

we beat
emotion
out of our little boys
and then wonder
why we have
emotionally broken men

He folds into himself.
Turns soft curves
into sharp edges.
Pounds his chest to make sure
his cage remains strong.
Releases a hurricane
when all he really needs
is the cleansing
of a quiet storm.

When I see a man
pacing.
punching.
screaming.
Doing anything
to keep from crying.
I wonder what terrible things
his mind
is saying to his heart.

L.E. Bowman

Do less,
he said.
I need to help you,
he said.
How can I be a man,
he said,
if you do not let me?

I want a lover who carries
soil in his hands
and water in his heart.
Who knows what it means to tend;
to only break ground when planting,
to always leave enough space
for the sun to do
her part.

L.E. Bowman

Why does society
boast
about hearts made of stone?
Like something
unfeeling and frozen
is superior
to something
warm and beating.

— *I will keep my bleeding heart.*

Machismo
is not a crown.

It is a cloak.

What are you hiding?

We worship her.
Crave her.
Place her on a pedestal of sexuality,
but as soon as she sees
what we see.
As soon as she loves herself,
as we love her.
We accuse her
of vanity.
of conceit.
Please tell me,
why are we allowed to see
the beauty
she radiates,
but she is not?

do not teach me
my sexuality
is the greatest power i have
and then shame me
when i use it

Sexism not only exists
in wolf whistles and unsolicited touches.
It exists
in ignored opinions.
in silenced voices.
in condescending smiles.

— *He does not have to touch you to disrespect you.*

even the softest whisper
will sound like a scream
when they expect you
to be silent

Erupt.
bleed fire and spew smoke.

Quake.
until your foundation cracks and your walls crumble.

Spin.
create tornados in your eyes;
let them peel and strip
until you are nothing but marrow and bone.

Until your sky
b r e a k s
into lavender and gold,
and calm finally
s
e
t
t
l
e
s
on your skin.

I am lightning on a quiet day.
My body is still,
but inside I am raging.

my voice is only thunder

wait for the storm

Just remember,
when you bite your tongue,
when they command silence
and you comply,
you are wrapping your fingers around the throats
of those who speak.

Just remember,
when your eyes shift and close,
when you pretend to not see what you see,
when your ears hear fireworks instead of bullet rounds,
and you continue to ignore the screams,
that it is you
who is now
the loudest sound.

That deafening boom of silence.
That thunderous roar of apathy.

don't allow your tongue
to become
so thick
with words you want to say
that you choke
each time
you try to speak

Raw emotion
is difficult for some to swallow.
Not everyone can stomach
veracity
dripping down their throat.

Like a girl
is not an insult.
not a praise.
It is a statement that holds no meaning.
no power.
For there are women
with the physicality of beasts,
with the strength of armies.
And there are men
with the delicacy of flowers,
with the innocence of children.
Such a declaration
cannot define.
cannot describe.
the complexity of individuals.
The mixture
of femininity.
of masculinity.
that resides in us all.

are you enough
for you
is the only question
you need to answer

She is condemned for using
needles to still her lines,
and filler to hide her cracks;
for reshaping
the unique parts of her
to fit an artificial mold,
when her only crime is aging
in a world
that worships youth
and places beauty
above all else.

What purpose does judgement serve
apart from validation
for the judger?
There is no one
more aware of her flaws
than the woman
who wears them.

his whistles and condescending words
hurt less
than her disapproving eyes and counterfeit smile

But you see,
they don't know what it's like
to fear your own body.
To question the desires you feel pulsing;
    the clenched thighs to make it stop.
Demure eyes and shaking hands
just trying to understand
why something
so visceral.
so natural.
so real.
is labeled as wrong.

There are women
who will never be seen as pure.
Skin too dark.
Urges too different.
An interest in the tingling in her stomach
instead of a fear of it.
The desire to learn a woman's body
instead of a man's,
> *but only when she's married,*
> *and only when he wants it.*

L.E. Bowman

You can't hold the pain
between your teeth
and expect it not to
seep into your tongue.
stain your blood.
plant roots in your bones.

This is how anger grows.

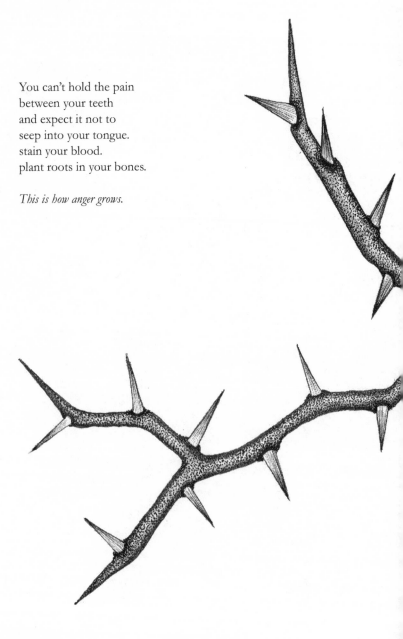

i wrapped myself
in thorns
and then hated everyone
who didn't want to
touch me

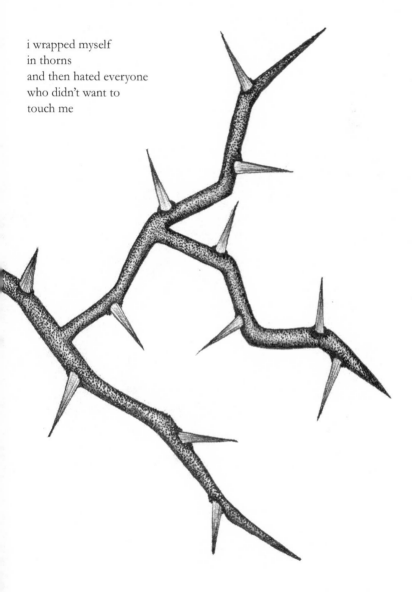

L.E. Bowman

At some point
the anger will define you;
your heat
no longer passion and hunger,
but hatred
clinging to skin.

At some point
the anger will become you;
your body
no longer heart and blood and bone,
but fire
longing to spread.

the problem with fire
is it must destroy
to stay alive

I am sick with fear
of people leaving,
so I hold the door wide open.
exit signs flashing.
palms gesturing.
See,
I say.
See,
I knew you would walk away.

you might find safety
behind your walls
but you will not
find peace

self-pity is the poison
we feed ourselves
when we are daunted by the work it takes
to grow

You must unlearn
the monologue of deprecation
you taught yourself.
Wash it
from your mind.
Rinse it
from your tongue.

how can you blame others
for your heartbreak
when you reject
that very heart
every
single
day

Parts of us
hunger for sadness.
Desolation.
Tragedy.
We fed them with darkness
for so long
they no longer know
how to consume the light.

I apologize to myself
daily,
but I rarely accept it.
I am still learning how to look myself
in the eyes
and say
you did okay.

The truth:
You are not flawless.

The lie:
You are supposed to be.

The heart will blossom with little assistance;
it's the mind that needs tending to.
Weeds pulled.
Seeds planted.
Tireless attention
given
every day.

— Only then will flowers grow.

I no longer cry,
    I gush.
I empty myself
until my body is frail and my limbs are weak.

But my eyes
—*my eyes*
are always clearer
than before.

You could be the brightest thing,
but I keep my secrets.
Wanting you in silence.
Kissing shadows.
Reaching with closed hands.

They hang heavy
in the air,
all the words I should tell you.

They make the room stink of
what if.

I want
to never have to question
your affection.
I want
to be so sure of
your love
that my anxieties
starve
and
die.

I don't need eruptions;
fire and lightning and waves.
I need the underbelly of the ocean.
Stillness and peace.
A quiet place to sink into
when it begins to rain.

I do not yet know
what it means to be a lover.
To lick wounds instead of skin.
To taste the salt of another's sadness.
To hold their beating heart
in my hands.

The truth is

I can
stand alone.
grow alone.
be alone.

But I do not want
to have to.

You expose me.
The raw and desperate pieces
I struggle to control.
The want.
The need.
The begging between my thighs.
The pounding in my chest.
The urging of my mind
screaming
for once foolish girl follow your heart.

I am still learning how to share.
How to get lost
without losing myself.
How to give
without giving myself away.

I didn't know
respect
until you hesitated
before touching me.
Your eyes searching.
Your hands hovering.
Your lips brimming
with a question
I was never asked before.

Yes, you may continue.

he called me intelligent
before
he called me beautiful

Some people aren't meant to fit.
They itch a little
—*rub*.
Make you feel
what you don't want to feel.
An uncomfortable tightness,
a suffocating pull,
like something about your skin
is no longer right;
like something inside of you
suddenly needs to
grow.

you introduced me to myself
and we fell in love with her
together

It was a sickening feeling,
being the one
on the other side of love.
Struggling to pull affection from memories.
Retracting from hands that once brought me peace.
Staring into eyes I thought held the world;
wondering when I realized the world was actually around me.

If I didn't understand
how my heart
could make all of these promises
and still
      somehow
get distracted along the way,

how could he?

it does not feel right
is
a reason

It was when I realized he was growing too;
struggling
through the same process
of expanding and breaking and expanding again,
that I found peace
in the endings.
That I found acceptance
in the realization
that we are all in constant motion,
and that it is often not love that is lacking,
but harmony.

I was softer after you.
Not just with the world
but with
myself.

L.E. Bowman

I am a mountain,
and he once was the sun,
bright
and warm on my skin.

I am a mountain,
and now he howls and screams
and tries to shake me,
but I
do not bend.

I am a mountain,
and he constantly changes from clear skies to storm,
from breeze to gale,
and what can I do but remain a mountain?
still.
steady.
unmoved.

I once was a mountain,
but then I realized
even mountains can be carved
by the wind.

If it hurts,
leave.

Not because
you no longer believe in love,
but because
you still do.

You're allowed to close the door on the world.
Take a minute, a day, a week
to breathe.
Ask for more time,
if that's what you need.

Boundaries
are not selfish.

Your comfort
means more
than their ego.

Life
may be difficult.
Timing and circumstance
and all the pain they bring,
may be difficult.
But love
—*love*
should always be
the easiest thing.

You
should not be used
to replace
him or her
or any other lovers
who came before.

You
should be
something new
entirely.

it is not
the fault of the skin
if the soul it holds
is unsettled

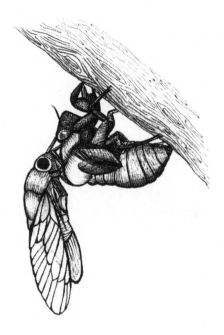

Did you think it would be easy?
The itching and the tearing,
that oppressive encasing,
when you become too much
and need to break free.

Unfolding isn't painless.
Stretching limbs.
Opening fingers.
Unveiling palms.
There is the stiffness and discomfort and that *pop*
when you finally extend,
but our bodies weren't made to remain stagnant;
to find a form and keep it.

Our bodies were made
to move.

Liberation wasn't about
cleansing myself;
it was about finally getting dirty.
It was about burying my hands in the muck
and not cringing when my nails became dark,
and the day collected in the lines of my palms.
It was about sweating and burning
and accepting uncertainty.
It was about jumping
with no notion of when
I might reach
the ground.

Do you not see
how strong you are?
All those times
the world
forced you to your knees
and still
you continue to rise.

Be so bold. so confident.
in your endeavors,
that people stop questioning you
and start
questioning themselves.

The heart, like any muscle,
only gets stronger when its threads are torn.
Do not fear the pain.
Instead, welcome the ache;
embrace the burning.
It is healing.
It is growth.

It is strength.

I've always had expansive roots;
a solid base,
which I nurtured
quietly
until it spread so deep and wide
that it was finally capable of supporting
everything that I am.
Now.
Ready.
Watch me bloom.

The Woman

Allow her to cry.
Hold her as she comes undone.
Be patient as the pieces crumble away.
She is not breaking.

She is opening.

the ocean in me has quieted
but i still
reek of salt

I knew I was closer to understanding what self-love meant
when you left and the deprecation did not come.
I didn't dwell on what I did or did not do.
I didn't stand in front of a mirror and question if the blurred version
staring back at me was the true representation of who I was.

Were my angles not right?
Did my moans not please you?
Was my mouth too sharp?
My mind too dull?

The answers to those questions no longer mattered.
I didn't need you to tell me I was beautiful
    —I knew I was.
I didn't need you to tell me I would find someone better
    —I knew I would.
Instead I mourned your departure like the loss of a childhood toy
that once brought comfort and happiness.
A piece of my past I would always remember,
but did not need.

When my gut twisted.
When the tears appeared and the breath
got lodged in my throat.

I started asking myself why.

When no answer
was the right answer.
When no move
got me where I wanted to go.

I started asking myself why.

When I was angry for no reason.
When I was angry for every reason.

I started asking myself why.

When the pain was everyone's fault
but mine.

I started asking myself *why*.

You are relearning
who you are
on your own.

Breathe.

Even rediscoveries
take patience
and time.

We always speak of the beauty of peaks,
but what of valleys.
Of the delicate flowers
that grow in the shadows of mountains.
Of the stones turned to diamonds
at their base.

I don't need to be the sun;
the center of it all.
Always present.
Always burning.

I mean, have you seen
how beautifully the fireflies dance
on warm summer nights?

Give me that peace.
That light.
That choice.
The ability to surround myself in darkness,
or to subtly, yet brilliantly
glow.

She tells me she wants me to still believe
in the existence of good men.
To still believe in love;
in the magic of it all.
But it isn't the men or the love or the magic
I now believe in.
It's the strength.
The courage she shows me
when she loses it all
and still
never loses hope.

If you want to see
true grit,
watch someone break.

Then watch as the pieces settle.
As hands begin moving.
As a new person
is made.

I'm not always a gentle woman.
My mouth is harsh,
bold, and unforgiving.
I get jealous of other women,
new loves,
old flames,
a prettier face.
I burn
more than I quench,
and my hands
scar
as much as heal,

but I am trying.

My arms are now
open
more than closed,
and my lips are learning
to speak gently.

And if you stay with me awhile
my nectar
has been know
to make
honey.

You can be whole
and still discovering pieces.
You can be lost
and still know where you are.

L.E. Bowman

You call them blemishes
    patchwork skin
formed from marks and spots and scars.
But what happens
    when you step back?
What happens
    when you view the whole?
Can you not picture the constellations?
Can you not see
that your body is not
stained
with imperfections,
but embellished
with stars.

When speaking to your body,
you do not
have to jump to
I love you.

I feel you.
I respect you.
And I am
learning
to love you
is an acceptable place
to start.

you hide
the remnants of war
that grace your skin
as if
they are not proof
that you fought
and won

Sit with yourself awhile.
Feel the ache in your bones;
the tremor in your heart.
Realize
your body
is in need of you
too.

You are strongest
when you think
you are weak.
When every breath hurts
and still
you breathe.

Healing begins with a decision.

Decide.

I wonder if the stars
envy each other
as we do.
If they become
so focused.
so blinded.
by the brilliance of their neighbors,
that they never see
the way they shine
on their own.

there is
what you think
you are

and then there is

more

.

i learned the most
about love
when the only person
i was falling in love with
was myself

The girl in me still exists.
I pass her in the hall on the nights when sadness sleeps over.
She welcomes the tears,
and I wipe them away.

What if this is Eden,
this body.
this life.
The earth and her wonders,
our mother.
With her bounty;
with the fruits of these hands
and this well-watered heart.
What if we are all too busy
reaching.
wanting.
to taste and devour.
Too consumed to see
that we already
have.
That we already
are.
all the things
we hunger for.

We tend to take care
of what we love.
Maybe that is why
so few of us
take care of ourselves.

I watched my mother shrink
while those around her continued to grow.
Giving. without taking.
Nursing. without feeding herself.
Letting the world
plow and reap
until her worth was wrapped too tightly around their fingers
to ever let go.
And who was to blame?
The world
for taking what was freely given,
or her
for thinking giving endlessly
would do anything
but tear her apart?

being selfless
without a sense of self
only leaves you with less

less connected
less fulfilled
less loved

No,
she whispers
to her growling stomach.
Not now,
she pleads
to her aching heart.
Later,
she murmurs
to her unsettled mind.
When,
they beg.
Soon,
she promises.

Just let me take care of them first.

how do you expect
to understand your pain
if you never let it
speak

There are days when the tears will come
endless
and without warning.
The ocean inside of you
violent
and impossible to soothe.
Sway with the waves;
allow the surge
to spill down your cheeks.
Storms
are to be weathered
not subdued.

I am a woman of seasons.
I burn.
I bloom.
I strike.
I turn to ice;
sometimes I melt away.

L.E. Bowman

How many nights
I have known
I will never see the sun again.
How many mornings
I have awoken
to it shining in my eyes.

Not every day
has to be better than the last.
Healing is the type of thing that
comes and goes,
wilts and grows.
A breath must leave you
before another can fill your lungs.

L.E. Bowman

Treat your pain
the way you treat your skin after a day of burning.
With gentle, cool hands
and the understanding
that it will sting.

You don't have to be fine,
but you have to be trying.

You can rest
as long as it's just
until you heal.
You can break
as long as you know
you will rebuild
again.

— *You are okay when you are not okay, for the healing is found in the breaking.*

Be patient.

You cannot remove a person
from your bones
while your hands are still shaking.

But you are trying now.
Replenishing tears with water instead of wine;
looking ghosts in the eye.
Opening curtains.
Unlocking doors.
Saying goodnight to the moon
and to the sun,
good morning.

There is a difference between
those who
do not love you,
and those who
do not know how.

The answer
is often found
in the way they
love themselves.

make your heart
so soft
even the most careless of hands
cannot break it

They tell me alchemy doesn't exist,
but I took this pain
and I turned it to gold;
this self-loathing to wine.
I learned how to transform destruction into growth;
how to take all these broken, chipped,
fragmented pieces
and make something
whole.

you are more
than the woman
he did not want

L.E. Bowman

You starved

for days.
for months.
for years.

and still you expect
to not feel weak.

Not all bravery is boastful.
Sometimes it moves in whispers.
Like the soft beat
of one foot
followed by another.

L.E. Bowman

Let me settle your mind:

You are enough.
He did know.
You did all that you could.
There will be another.

How many times you have died.
How many flowers
have grown from the decay.

Most of us aren't born into kindness,
raised with giving hands
and forgiving hearts.
Softness like that
is forged in battle;
empathy tended
by each new scar.

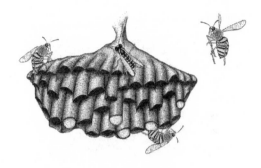

One summer my mother refused to use the gate to our pasture after a family of wasps built their dangling home in one of the bends of rusted metal.

They work so hard,
she said.
And they maintain it so well.
Even that storm last night,
even that storm last night didn't knock them down.
If they can survive that fury,
who I am
to destroy them now?

And besides,
she said,
I can always find another way around.

I was raised by the trees.
Hardened
by the stumps and weeds and rocks
in the ground.
Softened
by the wildflowers that grew
at my feet.

Return to your roots
when your limbs feel heavy.
Within the grit.
the soil.
that raised you,
you will find the strength
to grow again.

The greatest thing I ever did
was lose sight of perfection.
Forget it existed.
Stopped trying to gather it with my hands.
Stopped thinking it was tangible.
Definable.
Something I could buy.
Something
I could be.

my arms grew tired
from constantly reaching
so i wrapped them around myself
and allowed them
to rest

I traveled
beyond scaled slopes and past veiled folds.
Along dimly lit pathways and into unmapped hollows.
Where hidden within me
I discovered,
there is not only darkness
but also
light.

Be your last love.
Your final resting place.

The battle is not over
the moment you decide to love yourself.
Each day
your mind will still whisper,
are you sure?
Only now
    empowered
your heart will reply,
yes.

the days I feel the heaviest
are the days
i know
i am preparing
to bloom

Do it.
Fall in love.
Foolish.
Senseless.
Fearless.
Love.
Heartbreak will find you
whether you invite it or not,
so you might as well
enjoy the
high.

Your heart
is a precious, wild thing.
Do not let your mind
cage it.

L.E. Bowman

Show me a brave love;
a dirty love.
One dusted with soil from digging and planting.
One tenderly grown with sweat and tears.

If you do it right,
it's rarely soft and it's never clean.
There will be dirt stuck in your nails and your fingers will ache,
but your hands will never be empty.

Some days it will taste overdone,
burnt.
Others you will wonder if it's even cooked at all,
but that mix of nectar and brine
will always melt on your tongue.

It's more overcast than sunny,
with dark clouds in the distance
and that rumble you can feel in your gut.
But the rain will cleanse you.
And the sun,
the sun when it shines
will remind you.
Why it's always worth trying.
Why you'll never stop.

L.E. Bowman

I do not want a love
that takes my breath away.
I want a love
that fills my lungs.

Ask for what you want
always.
If they leave,
they were never going to give it to you.
But if they stay,

if they stay...

when you are so in bloom
that nectar
pours
from your fingers
and you can't even hate
the bees
for wanting to get a bite

My soul is stretching.
Purring.
Sighing.
Finally resting
after years of crying out.

If you want me to stay,
love me with open hands.
Let me feel the gentleness
of your palms.
Let me find comfort
in the knowledge
that I am free to leave.

Let me decide
I never want to.

He did not tame me.
He calmed with restless spirit;
he quieted my anxious mind.
And on the nights
when the wild beckoned,
we howled at the moon
together.

I do not want all of you.
I want you
to keep parts of you
for you.

But everything else.
I want.
Everything else.

the moment
you
felt more like home
than the house
i grew up in

We are captivated by the birth of love.
Enthralled
by the first few moments
when the world explodes in brilliant color.
When all hope and purpose seem to spring
from one person.
This is the alluring stage;
this is the fairytale,
but this is not love.
This is fascination.
This is chemicals flooding the brain that with time will expire.
It's the after that is love.
The sacrifice;
the compromise.

The I see you
fully.

The I want you
still.

you made a point
to kiss
my imperfections
every morning
because you knew
i never would

He loves the rivers I have flowing through me;
the lush forest that welcomes him in.
He says it makes him feel primal,
how I'm always open and inviting
and ready to be taken.
But what happens when my climate changes?
When my weather dries into deserts
and we both have to beg for rain.
When I have sand dunes instead of riverbeds
and my biota is barely awake.
Will my wilderness still tempt him then?
Will he find me just as beautiful,
this new landscape?

What a gift,
to see all seasons;
to be all seasons.
To feel the lust of spring
and the growth of summer.
To welcome autumn's fall
with open arms.
To smile during winter
at the memory
of how exquisitely you bloomed.

I do not love myself every day.

I still frown at the face in the mirror. Pull apart the pieces I hate.
    Poke and prod and pick.
Wonder how much softer my face would be with a smaller nose.
Clench my abs and twist until my waist curves as I was told it should.
I count the ways I have failed that day.
The wrong answers I gave.
The attitude I should try harder to hide.
I stare at blank pages and wonder why I cannot write.
I stare at pages full of words and wonder why I do.
My mistakes still haunt me. My future still scares me.
I still tie what-ifs to my ankles and wonder why I'm unable to move.

But I know these feelings are fleeting.
I know they only have power if I allow them to.
And just as happiness comes and goes,
so does pain.

I am soft and sharp
and whole and broken.
I am the home I know best
and a land I have yet to find.

Self-love is not a wall; not a shield to prevent pain.
It is a tool.
A way to cope. To accept. To grow.
To realize some love is fleeting, and the love of another is a gift.
Not a necessity.

there are parts of me
no one will ever love
so i love them
the most

Stop trying to make love beautiful;
allow it to just exist.
In its raw form; in its purest state.
Some days it will shine; some days it will barely glow.
Most days it will be quiet
—*simple*
only seen when looked for;
a reflection of the people it exists within.
Imperfect people
who rise.
who fall.
How can we expect something
that lives. that grows. that dies.
within us.
to behave differently than we do?

You are not here
to be loved.

You are here
to love.

There is something sacred in sunrises and sunsets.
In the warm promise of a new beginning;
in the cold beauty of an inevitable end.
In the constant cycle,
the undeniable consistency,
of both.

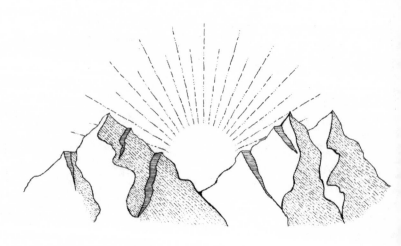

the take
is just as important
as the give

Do not let the quiver in your voice
deter you from speaking.

This is how waves are born.

I will raise my daughter
with *no*
sitting on her tongue,
and the taste of silence
foreign to her lips.
With the knowledge
that she is whole
alone
and that love
is only part
of the journey,
not the destination.

I do not want to strip you
of your masculinity.
I want to show you
femininity
is just as capable
and just as strong.

please tell me
how one woman
is more
woman
than another

we are all real women

My hands
will never touch you.
My eyes
will never see you.
But I hope
my words
reach you.
I hope they ignite
a fire
within you.
So we may
burn.
So we may
shine.
So we may
rise
together.

How much time we waste
attempting to extinguish each other.
Fighting to be first
in a world
that puts us all
second.

Fight for each other instead.

Carry the fear
in your hands
instead of in your heart.
Then you will be forced
to let it go
when you want to reach
for something else.

If you have a belly full of words
not ready for your lips,
write them.
Give them a backbone.
Watch as they grow limbs.
Support their first breath.
Wait.
Listen.
Soon you will hear them speak.

I am not
a daughter of the cosmos.
My mind
does not live above the clouds.
I have roots instead of wings,
and I crave the comfort of the soil
over the freedom of the sky.
Still,
I watched
the fleeting light of comets,
the burning brilliance of the sun,
and I wondered
if I should try to reach
my branches higher;
if I should try to shine
like the stars.

But then I realized
that the earth itself
is built
on fire.

The Evolution of a Girl

i put my pieces back
so beautifully
that i can't help
but thank
all the people
who broke me
apart

thank you